PARENTING WITH LOVE AND WISDOM

Charlene M. Mills

Table of contents

Chapter 1:

Parenting: Joy or Nightmare

Parenting can be a tough job, a thankless job. But it may also be really lovely. My children provide me more delight than I can possibly convey.

Does that imply it's easy? No. There are days I want to rage at my eldest and weep because of my smallest, as right now, since the little tyrant in my life — as my toddler — is screaming as I type this. But it isn't all horrible, and it doesn't have to be. With a few key modifications, everyone may aspire toward becoming a "happy parent." Here is what we know about joyful parenting. While the word "happy parent" may sound broad and sophisticated, we can surely agree that the principle underpinning it is really very basic.

Happy parents are folks who find delight in most days, if not every day. They know there is a silver lining to every cloud, and happy parents enjoy their role as parents. Happy parents breathe. They pause and smell the flowers. They tell themselves that their screaming toddler will one day be an angry adult who sticks up for herself. They know that dinnertime ending in tears is simply one moment in a future that involves many, many wonderful evenings. Of course, this thought may look commonplace, like filler or fluff, particularly if you're not used to this style of thinking. It's also easier said than done on those tough days when nothing seems to be going right. But shifting your thinking could have long-term health benefits. Yes, happiness may be helpful for your heart in more than an abstract approach. A tiny research of 40 women from 2011 indicated that those who reported having more optimistic attitudes recovered from stress quicker, with their blood pressure returning to normal faster. An prior study from 2003 Trusted Source investigated 334 individuals and revealed that those who reported having higher pleasant emotions were less likely to catch a cold virus when exposed.

Are there secrets to happy parenting?
According to a 2009 research, despite stress and challenges, parenthood might boost your life satisfaction. However, this is influenced by individual factors, like your personality. Simply having kids isn't the way to happiness. And it's not just your attitude - other conditions, including your marital status, economic situation, and political limitations come into play when influencing parental happiness. Trusted Source of various nations found that those who resided in regions with higher parental leave, occupational flexibility, and other supporting policies for parenting had superior happiness. While it would be fantastic if we all got the support we need, on all levels, certain things are beyond our

control to alter. So what can you handle when it comes to being a happy parent?

Happy parents don't necessarily do anything unusual to "be happy." Instead, persons who wish to discover more enjoyment in parenting embrace a conviction that they may uncover the wonderful, even when situations are unpleasant or they aren't genuinely feeling that cheerful themselves. There are no certainties for happiness, and attaining parental bliss doesn't suggest that you'll automatically be a happy person. But it doesn't damage to concentrate on the good. This may not be your default pick, and that's OK. Not everyone can readily look on the bright side. That said, there are things you can do to boost your happiness.

Realize that things don't have to be perfect — and that you don't have to be perfect — for them to be good. You just have to try. You simply have to be pleased with good enough. Happy parents embrace the wonderful, the horrible, and the ugly. They recognize that one argument, terrible tantrum, or lost opportunity isn't the end of the world.

Chapter 2

Setting limits through thinking words
Love and Logic parenting is a law-and-order philosophy. Just because we recommend that parents shy away from issuing orders and imposing their solutions on their kid's problems does not mean we give license to all sorts of misbehavior. The process is to allow our kids to mess up, and not drive home the lesson of their misdeeds with words. Be slow to lecture, and never tell the child what he has just learned. Instead, give guidance, but allow them to think for themselves. Making enforceable statements and giving choices, forces that thinking back on them.

Building Walls That Don't Crumble

How do we set limits on their behavior without telling them what to do? Limits are crucial to what we are trying to do and our kids need the security of boundaries in order to make those decisions. From the time our kids are infants, we set limits for them, limits that put boundaries around their behavior. Some parents build walls in the form of firm limits for their children; others leave their kids to feel insecure and afraid by providing few limits, or limits that crumble easily.

Kids seem most secure around parents who are strong, who don't allow the limits they place on their kids to crumble. Conversely, children lose respect for adults who cannot set limits and make them stick. Quite simply put, kids who misbehave without having to face the consequences become brats. Children who have limits placedced on them in loving ways become secure enough to not only deal effectively with their own emotions but form satisfying relationships with others as well. These relationships allow children to develop self-confidence. These children are easier to teach, spend less time misbehaving, and they grow up to be responsible adults. Lack of firm limits lead to low self-esteem and the behavior follows accordingly.

How to Talk to a Child

For many parents, setting limits means issuing commands and backing up those limits with more commands spiced with sternness and anger. They think that every time they say something to their kids, they are setting limits, and the louder their voice gets and the more often they repeat it, the firmer the limits become. This may have immediate results, but the long-term prognosis is not very good. Love and Logic parents insist on respect and obedience, just as command-oriented parents do. But when Love and Logic parents talk to their children, they take a different approach. Instead of the fighting words of command-oriented parents, they use thinking words. Thinking words, used in question form and expressed in enforceable statements, are one of the keys to parenting with Love and Logic parents. They place the responsibility for thinking and decision making on the children.

What is the difference between "fighting words" and "thinking words"? The former is an order and the second is a contemplative statement. "Fighting words" are the ones in which we challenge our kids and offer a negative consequence for them not following through with a positive response. E.g., "Don't you talk to me in that tone of voice!" "Thinking words" are ways to think of enforceable statements that make kids think for themselves. For example, "You sound upset. I'll be glad to listen when your voice is as soft as mine is."

Children learn better from what they tell themselves than from what we tell them. Kids are more prone to believe something that comes from inside their own heads: they choose an option, they do the thinking, they make the choice, and the lesson sticks.

Would you rather carry your coat or wear it?

Would you rather put on your boots now or in the car?

Would you rather play nicely in front of the television or be noisy outside?

Kids fight against commands and the difference between the thinking words and fighting words are subtle. More control by the parent is perceived as less control by the child. They exert themselves to regain the control they see slipping away.

The Threat Cycle

The temptation to use threats is great because we desperately want to assail our kids with commands and threats to limit their behavior. Simply put, using threats doesn't make us feel like the wimp we feel like if we whimper, cry, beg, or plead with our kids, and threats sometimes work.

Some kids respond to threats, and others do not. They may do as they are told, but they are angry with the person who gave the order. Or they may perform the task in a way that is unsatisfactory simply to regain some of the control they had taken from them. Either way, they are breaking the limit we are trying to set. Our goal is to use thinking words and enforceable statements.

Passive-Aggressive Behavior

When children are commanded to do something they don't like, they often respond with passive-aggressive behavior. Kids know they must comply with the order or else reap punishment. They channel their anger in a way that will hurt their parents, so subtly that the parents don't know they are being hurt. They will make it sting sharply enough so that those parents will think twice before giving that order again.

The book uses the example of the girl who was responsible for doing the dishes, but she would procrastinate until it was too late at night and was in a rush the next morning. When mom gave the ultimatum, the daughter did the dishes, but broke a glass "accidentally" in order to get back at mom. The daughter's subtle message was "You better think twice before you force me to do the dishes again."

Passive-Resistive Behavior
When kids react to parental demands with passive-resistive behavior, they resist without telling the parent they are resisting. The resistance is in their actions, not their words. For example, when a parent tells a child to do something, the child responds by claiming he forgot the request or with less than instantaneous obedience. The attitude is "I'll comply, but I'll do it on my own terms." A sure sign of passive-resistant behavior in children is parental frustration. Parents may be frustrated without having passive-resistant children, but all passive-resistant children have frustrated parents.

We Would Rather Think Than Fight
Fighting words invite disobedience; they actually challenge the child to be disobedient. When they are used, we are drawing a line in the sand and daring the kids to cross it, and they will fight the limits we impose by using the fighting words. Fighting words include three types of commands:
Telling the kids what to do, "You get to work on the lawn right now."
Telling our kids what we will not allow, "You are not going to talk to me that way!"
Telling our kids what we won't do for them, "I'm not letting you out of this house until you clean your room."

When we issue commands we are calling our kids to battle and in many cases these are battles we cannot win. Why not simply steer away from words that cannot be challenged or fought? Limits can be set much more effectively when we are not fighting with our kids. It has been clinically proven that kids who are thinking cannot fight us at the same time. Love and logic parents make statements with enforceable thinking word telling their kids:

What we will allow: "Feel free to join us for your next meal as soon as the lawn is mowed."

What we will do: "I'll be glad to read you a story as soon as you have finished your bath."

What we will provide: "You may eat what is served, or you may wait and see if the next meal appeals to you more."

The word "no" is the biggest fighting word in the parental arsenal of commands. For two-year olds, parents us the word "No" over three-fourths of the time. Children tire of hearing it. The rule of "no" is to use it as little as possible, but when we do use, we mean business. At other times use a "yes" to something else. For example, "Yes, you may watch television as soon as your chores are done." By using thinking words, we are able to set limits on our children's behavior without telling them what to do. For example, if we want the lawn mowed before the next meal, we set that limit by offering them the choice: of mowing the lawn and eating, or not doing the lawn and not eating. In the real world, we get our job done, get paid and then we eat. When we give our children the right to make decisions, there is no anger for them to rebel against. Nobody is doing their thinking for them and the limit is established. "Yes" is always more fun to say than "no" if we are healthy and do not get a kick out of controlling others. Loving parents who encourage responsibility early are less likely to get into these hassles:

"Can I have __________?"
"Honey, if anyone deserves that__________, it is you. Buy it!"
"I don't have the money."
Sorry about that. It is like that a lot for me too. I guess then you will not buy it."

Mean What You Say, and Say What You Mean.Just as quickly as kids learn the limits, they will test them. They actually need to test them to make sure that the limits are firm enough to provide the needed security. They need to find out if we mean what we say and if we are going to stand firm on our word or not. Some will test the limits with anger or guilt, some are sneaky, and others will fake forgetfulness as a means of testing parental resolve. They will pout, complain, stomp around, run to their rooms, whine, or talk back. Using guilt is one of their most effective tools.

The kids will not like the Love and Logic methods; they would prefer the ways and will revert to them at every opportunity. The limit is the choice of the child: of course, they are hungry if they chose to put off the next meal because they did not mow the lawn. The hunger is a natural consequence to their action. If you don't work, you don't eat. If we relent, we demolish the meaning of those consequences. We set up a crumbling limit for our children. If we get angry at them for the choice they made or if we rail into them with an "I told you so", we also present a crumbling limit. They then have ample reason to direct their anger toward their parents instead of themselves. Using enforceable thinking words, giving choices, displaying no anger, these are the ingredients for establishing firm limits with our kids.

Chapter 3

Addressing Strong willed behavior

Strong-willed children may be rigid, obstinate, and likely to become emotionally locked in irritation and fury if they don't get their way. They might be opinionated and hyper-focused on accomplishing things their way ("the proper way"). They might appear unrelenting in pursuit of power and control. But for all this, when they acquire humility, compassion, and self-control, these youngsters may mature into excellent leaders. The Bible teaches us, "For the time, every discipline looks painful rather than pleasant, but eventually it bears the quiet fruit of righteousness to those who have been taught by it" (Hebrews 12:11). (Hebrews 12:11). We must discipline and teach our strong-willed children so that they may develop into the fullness of what God wants for them. Training involves intentionality via objectives. Creating structure requires time, practice, and hard effort. What are you educating your strong-willed youngster to seek and do? I see strong-willed youngsters as wild stallions eager to gallop and go no matter what. You get to teach and guide your kid toward what God has in store for them inside the Kingdom of God! As the Bible says, "Discipline your son, and he will give you peace; he will provide happiness to your heart" (Proverbs 29:17). (Proverbs 29:17).

be:

1. Be Calm

Calmness lets you tap into your intuition and parental intelligence. It enables you to react to their beliefs rather than their behavior. For example, your kid may have an outburst, but instead of instantly criticizing the behavior, you might attempt to understand what he sees and desires. Help him learn how to better understand what he's feeling or more successfully seek what he wants. Your tranquility helps calm a turbulent strong-willed child's brain.

Make your tranquillity infectious and not your child's emotions.

2. Be Clear

Clarity helps you enforce limits rather than waste your time and energy nagging and fighting. Tell your youngster the rules and consequences - positive and negative – and reaffirm what you have discussed. It's a terrific idea to have your youngster take an active role in setting the rules and punishments. You may employ the essential phrase, "What do you hear me saying?" Take time to make sure things have been stated clearly.

3. Be Consistent

Consistency helps strong-willed youngsters understand that being in control is not up for grabs. While it's not always simple, the parents must be unified in their approach. Otherwise, the youngster rapidly recognizes that authority and power are uncertain and split. Strong-willed youngsters react to competence and confidence.

4.FollowThrough\Strong-willed youngsters want to know that you mean what you say. They respect and trust decisive authority. When you follow through, it is as if you're placing money in the Bank of Trust between you and your kid.

5. Delegate Some Control

Give your kid the opportunity to earn an acceptable level of decision-making privilege in your family — she can't just demand it. For example, you may delegate her responsibility over deciding what path you will cycle, but not if you're going riding. She could also come up with realistic ideas to clean and maintain the property.

6. Teach and Reinforce Empathy and Humility

Most crucial, educate and reinforce empathy and humility early and frequently. Help them learn to listen and care about others. Talk about what it looks like, to be honest, faithful, loyal, true, ethical, and loving and supportive of others. When strong-willed youngsters learn how to be empathetic and modest (two core relationship skills), they may become outstanding leaders. Help them realize the worth of other people — their views, opinions, and well-being — as they learn to influence rather than dominate. If their brain becomes trapped, help them break free. You might remark, "It appears like your brain is stuck. I'm hiring a brain tow truck to get your brain unstuck so you may be free." Or, when your kid is emotionally all over the place, you may remark, "Your brain is racing around the room, and we need to catch it and put it back in the driver's seat. It seems your body is driving without a driver." Young, strong-willed youngsters also do well with diversions. For example, if they are fixated on a subject, give them a random fact like, "Did you know some cats are allergic to humans?" Or you might ask a random inquiry, "How many teeth do sharks have?"

Strong-Willed Individuals Can Have Historic Impact

I adore examining the wonderful contributions in history by strong-willed people. Thomas Edison (creator of the light bulb) observed, "I never allow myself to feel disheartened under any circumstances.

I remember that after we had run hundreds of tests on a given project without addressing the issue, one of my colleagues, after we had undertaken the crowning experiment and it had been a failure, voiced frustration and contempt over our having failed 'to find out anything.' I cheerily informed him that we had learned something, because we had learned for a fact that the item couldn't be done that way and that we would have to attempt some other approach."

Having a stubborn will can get us through discouragement, obstacles, and moments of failure. Although parenting strong-willed children can be demanding, it can also be incredibly gratifying and powerful. However, it also involves your growth in adaptability, respect, intentionality, steadfast love, boundaries, graceful forgiveness, and gratitude. What an incredible opportunity for personal growth as you guide an influencer and contributor in God's kingdom. When educated with patience and firm, loving supervision, strong-willed youngsters may become life-changing leaders like Paul, Peter, Esther, and Daniel in the Bible

Chapter 4

Sensitivity understanding how they feel

Do you have children whose responses appear to be excessive: for example, when they witness something upsetting, they weep for hours afterward? Do they become angry about what seems to be the slightest of things and sometimes nothing at all? Or, do you have children that appear to seldom get angry or communicate how they are feeling? The degree to which your children are emotionally sensitive is an intrinsic aspect of their character. An individual's temperament consists of 10 features and is what makes all children distinct in how they react to the environment around them. Understanding your children's temperament will allow you to raise them in the most efficient manner possible.
What is Emotional Sensitivity?

Emotional sensitivity refers to the ease or difficulty with which your children react emotionally to different events. This attribute is tested on two scales. The first scale evaluates how tuned in your youngsters are to their own emotions. Some youngsters are extremely sensitive emotionally to their own emotions and experience things very profoundly, while others do not appear to be aware of what they are experiencing at all.

The second scale assesses how sensitive your children are to others' feelings and emotions. Some youngsters are tuned in to what is going on for others while other children seem to be non-responsive to what they perceive emotionally around them. It is crucial to note that some children might be high on one scale of emotional sensitivity and low on the other. They may be exceedingly conscious of their sentiments, even to the point of being self-absorbed, yet not aware of other people's feelings, and vice versa. Determine how emotionally sensitive your children are to assess your children's degree of emotional sensitivity you might use the following questions to assist you. Track your responses on the following two scales from one to five:

Emotional Sensitivity, to self
Are your youngsters able to convey precisely what they are feeling?
When viewing a frightening movie or reading a sad novel, do they have responses that appear to be excessive or "over the top"?
Does your youngster weep a lot and have a hard time "letting things go"?
Does your kid become too agitated when someone punishes, criticizes or
talks harshly to them?
No
Yes

1   2   3   4   5

Unaware   of   own   feelings
Feels Strongly

emotionally sensitive

If the bulk of your replies falls toward the right side of either or both scores, then you have children who are more emotionally sensitive. This indicates that your children have a propensity to exhibit feelings such as sadness, grief, concern, embarrassment, fear, empathy, or rage more straightforwardly, even more dramatically, than those who are less emotionally sensitive. The idea is not to ignore their sentiments; instead, to educate children on how to communicate their intense responses in socially acceptable ways. These youngsters will frequently discuss with you how they feel about every little thing. They may feel and express any injustices extremely intensely, such as those linked to their siblings and "fair" treatment.

Do not take their passionate feelings too personally. They tend to hang on to sentiments far longer than others, which may be \ very challenging for parents. Teach children how to forgive and forget, so they can \slearn to move on and not linger on sentiments. Highly emotionally sensitive youngsters might get overwhelmed when they see visuals presenting emotionally charged issues. Parents may need to manage their children's watching of media or events that are too scary or depressing. The good side of having children that are more emotionally sensitive, particularly towards others, is that they frequently tend to be a lot more caring and compassionate.

As adults, they often do well in careers in the helping professions, and they can be very sensitive writers.

Emotional Sensitivity, to others

Do your children seem to notice when others are upset or hurt?

Do they appear to "feel what others are feeling"?

Do your children exhibit a lot of empathy or compassion for people who are upset?

No

Yes

| 1 | 2 | 3 | 4 | 5 |

Insensitive to others' feelings Emotionally tuned in.   Feels Strongly

If, on the other hand, most of your answers to the questions above fall toward the left side of the scale, then you have children who are less emotionally sensitive. These youngsters seldom feel angry even under difficult conditions and tend not to make a "big deal" about things.

They typically do not notice and are oblivious of how others are feeling and occasionally they even can be labeled insensitive or self-centered. These youngsters need to learn to discern what others are experiencing and frequently they require support in comprehending their feelings. Parents may assist by identifying these emotions for their children, talking about feelings, and promoting the expression of their children's sentiments. Everyday experiences, like watching the news or a movie, reading a book together, or shopping, maybe fantastic chances to discuss your thoughts and emotions, and help your children recognize and speak about their feelings and responses.

Things Parents Can Do
Understand that emotional sensitivity is a component of your children's inborn disposition. Avoid negatively categorizing your children who may be more emotionally sensitive as a "whiner" "cry-baby" or "selfish." Instead, use descriptive, more positive adjectives like

"more sensitive," "tenderhearted," "intense" and "aware of their feelings."

Acknowledge your children's temperament and enable them to understand their disposition. Learn to respect your children's unique way of being so you can understand their passionate responses and behaviors and avoid humiliating or embarrassing them for being who they are. Teach youngsters the language to use to describe more correctly and responsibly how they are feeling. Learn to work together. Understand how your temperament fits or does not match with your children's temperament and establish tactics to support each other. Send messages to your children that assist them to recognize their unique being and help them to feel good about who they are.

"You have really strong feelings."

"You express yourself strongly."

"You care a lot about other people."

"You are highly conscious of how other people are feeling about things."
"You know what you are experiencing and prefer to tell me about it."
"You may experience what you are experiencing and then move on."
"You can learn to grasp other people's emotions and perspectives."

Sensitive youngsters are everywhere. Their numbers are believed to be between 15 to 20 percent of youngsters in a North American culture, yet they are frequently misinterpreted or not identified as highly sensitive. What does it imply when we say a youngster is "sensitive" and how would you know whether your child is among them?. To make sense of sensitivity, it is best to start with knowing what it is not. It is sometimes mistaken for a youngster who has strong emotional responses or whose emotions appear to be more quickly harmed. Sometimes it is mistaken for a youngster who looks to be more attentive to others' needs or who is gentle or kind. While children with sensitivity may demonstrate some of these qualities, they are not typical of all sensitive kids, nor do they help us grasp what is at the base of their unusual way of being in the world. Sensitive youngsters are characterized as individuals who have elevated responsiveness to the environment via their senses. It may be via any sense—touch, taste, smell, sight, or hearing—and it is unique to each kid. It also occurs on a continuum, with some kids being more affected by touch and scent while others may be affected visually or by another sense.

Talking senses
While no two sensitive kids are alike, their enhanced receptivity to sensory information leaves them without a "skin" against the world. Things can feel too much, too big, too cold, too loud, too hot, too smelly, too painful, and too

overwhelming. In other words, they might easily feel overwhelmed by stimuli and this can stir them up emotionally. They are also prone to be more aroused and reactive in surroundings that stir up their senses. For example, I recall witnessing a youngster race for the door in his Mommy & Me music class every time the volume began to grow. The cacophony of noises was neither calming nor entertaining but instead rushed into him, filling him, and overpowering him.

As he reflexively ran for the door to flee, some people perceived him as disrespectful or belligerent, but in actuality, he was just overwhelmed. It is vital to regard sensitivity not as a pathology but as part of the variability in human temperament. Sensitivity doesn't appear to be a mistake when you look at it from an evolutionary standpoint. You may discover sensitivity in other animal species (even in fruit flies!) offering credence to the hypothesis that it is not a mistake but possibly adapted in some manner. What is evident is that sensitive youngsters require grownups to "get them" and to take care of them. This is true for any youngster, but much more so for the sensitive ones among us.

How do you know if your child is sensitive? Sensitive kids reveal themselves soon enough to their adults. The child will seem more easily triggered or comforted through a sense, or combination of them. In certain circumstances, overly-stimulating settings may prove to be provocative or distressing to young ones. Likewise, the sensitive kid may also find comfort in specific senses: for example, a child with tactile sensitivity may only sleep when they are held or caressed, while one with an auditory sensitivity may enjoy hearing your calm voice as they go asleep. Sensitive kids often seem to have unusual alertness even as babies. They may sometimes be described as "old souls" or the ones who watch everything. They can sometimes display exceptional memory and become preoccupied with their thoughts. Their questions are often probing and reveal a unique way of looking at the world. They might have a variety of interests or can become intensely engaged on one topic in particular.

Sensitive kids are generally characterized by adults as being intense, enthusiastic youngsters with great ideas and aspirations. When they are joyful they can infect a room with their exuberance just as when they are sad, they can fill a room with hurricane-force levels of anger. As the mom of two sensitive kids, I have seen first-hand what comes with caring for them. One of my daughters is highly sensitive and sees too much at times which surfaced when she was 18 months old as she shouted at visitors to stop staring at her. It was weird to be seen by someone she didn't know, and their attention was unwelcome and scary. She was also the same youngster who would never sing or dance in front of other parents at school because "they were all strangers." Her visual awareness gives her skills like the capacity to memorize details, detect patterns, and develop creative and innovative designs—like her "candy wall" when she was three. At the same time, it may become unpleasant when there is too much input, notably in terrifying movies with noises, sights, and tension.

Research suggests there is often a genetic component to this enhanced receptivity, or that it may be due to birth practices, as well as prenatal experiences. Genetics has a key effect in defining the strength or prominence of each afflicted sense. As indicated, it may be any combination of the five conventional senses, or internal senses like the vestibular (balance) system, proprioceptive sense (movement), or the complex sensing apparatus we call "the gut." Parents need just pay attention to what stirs a youngster up and evaluate how much is too much for them to figure out which combination of senses are amplified. The key to understanding sensitive youngsters is to not hold their large responses against them but to realize how they are being touched by the environment around them, and how to deal with them successfully.

Providing a feeling of security
Brain growth is a fantastic thing—especially in young children. With perfect settings, a sensitive child's brain will grow such that it can gradually manage and comprehend sensory information. They may build neuronal circuitry that can handle the sensory overload and discover strategies to adjust for too much stimulation. In other words, nature provides a remedy for a child's sensitivity, but it requires our aid for them to inwardly nurture these solutions. If we can create ideal developmental conditions for a child, then nature can take

over and grow the child up through their sensitivity.

How to respond to sensitive kids:
1, Strong, loving adult relationships
Sensitive kids need strong caring relationships with adults who convey to them that they are not too big, too difficult, or too much of anything. Sensitive youngsters are frequently more conscious of the fragility inherent to relationships; that is, if you give someone your heart, they may harm you. It is emotionally vulnerable to trust someone, to grow close, and depend on them for caretaking. Adults need to take a firm lead and persuade a kid they can trust them, particularly when it comes to coping with a child's blunders or problematic behaviors. Separation-based discipline such as time-outs, 1-2-3 magic, or punishments may frequently go too far and promote uneasiness in relationships. Attachment based and developmentally-friendly punishment is

crucial to being an emotionally secure caregiver in the hearts of our sensitive youngsters. Little things may go a long way in building a bond with a sensitive youngster.

It may be the simple things we remember, the care we take to draw them out and hear their story, and all the ways we convey that we appreciate being with them. Relationships are vital to all youngsters but sensitive ones don't "suffer fools gladly" and they typically wait to see whether someone can be trusted before giving them their heart. We need to try to win their confidence and be patient until we are there. Whoever cares for a sensitive child will need to work on a relationship with them to get them to follow and take their cues. This is true in a daycare setting as well as at school with their instructors.

2. Know when to guard against and when to promote exposure

If a youngster does not have thick skin to shield them from sensory overload, then it will fall to its grownups to compensate for this. We may start by modifying the child's surroundings. For example, some kids prefer white noise to cancel out environmental stimuli or may benefit from headphones.

Caregivers need to be patient and accept that their child may not want to engage in activities that are overwhelming such as playing with a lot of kids or music classes. While it is necessary to limit arousal and stimulation when appropriate, it is equally crucial to think about whether and when you can gently introduce sensitive youngsters to the things that are overwhelming for them. For example, one mother had a kid with a lot of sensitivities and loud noises were especially tough. She begged her mother not to walk by a construction site near their house because of the loud sounds of the big trucks and "diggers." The mother took note that this was a challenge for her daughter and took a different route as they walked to school each morning. One morning she told to her daughter, "We are only going to briefly pass past the building site and I want you to put your hands on your ears so that it won't be too loud for you." As they rushed past, her daughter spotted the diggers and the hole in the ground and got captivated. As the week went on, the mother continued to go by the building site with her kid, looking and ultimately stopping. One day her daughter pulled her hands off her ears and listened, and finally, she was able to go by the location without feeling overwhelmed. What sensitive kids need is an adult who understands them and who knows when to shield them and when, and how, to gently and patiently encourage exposure to the hard things.

3. Make room for their emotions and tears
Sensitive kids can be stirred up by the world around them and this can create big

emotions inside of them that need to be released. The best thing we can do for them is to help them express feelings through words, play, or through their tears. Sometimes we need to encourage play that will draw out their frustration, fears, or desires. It is often easier to face things in play when it isn't for real or can't hurt you. If we are to move a sensitive child to their words or tears, they will need to trust us and see that our relationship is unwavering even when they are having a hard time. When we have to deal with difficulties with their behaviors we may make more progress outside of the event. They may be more receptive and able to hear us when we speak to them when they are less worked up and feeling close to us. Sometimes kids may not want to speak about concerns or tell us they can't recall. We may just tell them we will make it quick, and simple, and it won't hurt but we just need to say a few words. We may need to guide them into the sensitive area but if we fail to do so then they will have a tougher difficulty building a connection with the emotions inside of them.

If there were a secret to caring for sensitive youngsters it would be to know that they frequently behave in congruence with the sensory world that resides inside of them. They are not attempting to give us a hard time—they are just having a hard time. While there are problems brought by their sensitivity, there are also blessings, which caretakers learn to identify as emanating from the same source. If we can have these things in mind while interacting with them and welcome them to relax in our care, then we will be able to become the powerful caregivers they require.

Chapter 5

Parenting your Children in love and Wisdom

Raising kids is one of the hardest and most satisfying occupations in the world — and the one for which you may feel the least equipped. These 9 child-rearing practices will help you feel more satisfied as a parent.

1. Boost Your Child's Self-Esteem

Kids start forming their concept of self as newborns when they perceive themselves via their parents' eyes. Your tone of voice, your body language, and your every emotion are absorbed by your kids. Your words and actions as a parent affect their growing self-esteem more than anything else. Praising successes, whatever minor, will help children feel proud; letting youngsters do things autonomously will make them feel competent and powerful. By contrast, disparaging words or comparing a youngster unfavorably with another can make kids feel worthless. Avoid making loaded comments or using words as weapons. Comments like "What a dumb thing to do!" or "You behave more like a baby than your tiny brother!" create harm just as physical strikes do. Choose your words wisely and be sympathetic. Let your kids know that everyone makes mistakes and that you still love them, even when you don't appreciate their conduct.

2. Catch Kids Being Good

Have you ever stopped to think about how many times you respond adversely to your kids on a given day? You may find yourself criticizing significantly more frequently than praising. How would you feel about a manager who treated you with that much negative counsel, even if it was well-intentioned? The more effective method is to catch them doing something right: "You made your bed without being asked – that's amazing!" or "I was watching you play with your sister and you were

quite patient." These words will do more to promote good conduct over the long term than frequent scoldings. Make a point of finding something to praise every day. Be generous with incentives – your love, hugs, and congratulations may work wonders and are frequently rewarded enough.
Soon you will realize you are "developing" more of the behavior you would want to see.

3. Set Limits and Be Consistent With Your Discipline
Discipline is required in every home. The purpose of discipline is to help youngsters select appropriate actions and gain self-control. Kids may challenge the restrictions you make for them, but they need those limits to develop into responsible individuals. Establishing home rules helps youngsters understand your expectations and develop self-control. Some restrictions may include: no TV until

school work is done, and no hitting, name-calling, or nasty taunting permitted.

You may wish to have a system in place: one warning, followed by repercussions such as a "time out" or loss of rights. Typical error parents make is failing to follow through with the consequences. You can't chastise kids for talking back one day and disregard it the next. Being consistent teaches what you anticipate.

4. Make Time for Your Kids

It's frequently challenging for parents and kids to get together for a family dinner, much alone spend meaningful time together. But there is probably nothing youngsters would want more. Get up 10 minutes earlier in the morning so you may have breakfast with your kid or leave the dishes in the sink and take a stroll after supper. Kids who aren't receiving the attention they desire from their parents frequently act out or misbehave since they're guaranteed to be noticed that way.

Many parents find it pleasant to arrange a family time with their kids. Create a "special night" each week to be together and allow your kids to help select how to spend the time. Look for alternative ways to connect - put a letter or something special in your kid's lunchbox. Teens tend to require less undivided attention from their parents than younger youngsters. Because there are fewer windows of opportunity for parents and teenagers to get together, parents should do their best to be present when their teen does indicate a want to chat or engage in family activities. Attending concerts, games, and other activities with your adolescent conveys care and enables you to get to know more about your kid and his or her pals in essential ways. Don't feel bad if you're a working parent. It is the countless small things you do — preparing popcorn, playing cards, window shopping — that kids will remember.

5. Be a Good Role Model

Young kids learn a lot about how to behave by observing their parents. The younger they are, the more clues they absorb from you. Before you lash out or blow your top in front of your kid, think about this: Is that how you want your child to act when angry? Be mindful that you're always being observed by your kids. Studies have indicated that children who strike generally have a role model for aggressiveness at home. Model the characteristics you desire to see in your kids: respect, friendliness, honesty, compassion, and tolerance. Exhibit selfless conduct. Do things for other individuals without expecting a return. Express appreciation and give praises. Above all, treat your kids the way you want other people to treat you.

6. Make Communication a Priority

You can't expect them to do everything just because you, as a parent, "say so.

" They want and deserve answers as much as adults do. If we don't take time to explain, youngsters will begin to worry about our beliefs and intentions and if they have any substance. Parents who reason with their kids assist them to comprehend and learn in a nonjudgmental manner. Make your expectations clear. If there is a problem, discuss it, share your thoughts, and allow your kid to work on a solution with you. Be careful to mention repercussions. Make ideas and provide alternatives. Be receptive to your child's recommendations as well. Negotiate. Kids who engage in choices are more inclined to carry them out.

7. Be Flexible and Willing to Adjust Your Parenting Style
If you regularly feel "let down" by your child's conduct, possibly you have unreasonable expectations. Parents who believe in "shoulds" (for example, "My kid should be potty-trained by now") can find it

beneficial to study up on the issue or to chat with other parents or child development professionals. Kids' settings influence their behavior, thus you may be able to modify that behavior by changing the environment. If you find yourself continuously saying "no" to your 2-year-old, look for methods to change your settings so that fewer items are off-limits. This will generate less irritation for both of you. As your kid matures, you'll progressively have to adapt your parenting technique. Chances are, what works with your child now won't work as well in a year or two.

Teens tend to look less to their parents and more to their peers for role models. But continue to give advice, encouragement, and appropriate punishment while enabling your adolescent to gain greater freedom. And grasp every possible time to build a connection!

8. Show That Your Love Is Unconditional

As a parent, you're accountable for disciplining and directing your kids. But how you offer your remedial advice makes all the difference in how a youngster absorbs it. When you have to approach your kid, avoid accusing, you condemning, or fault-finding, which undermines self-esteem and may lead to resentment. Instead, attempt to love and encourage, even while scolding your kids. Make sure they know that while you want and expect better next time, your love is there no matter what.

9. Know Your Own Needs and Limitations as a Parent

Face it - you are an imperfect parent. You have strengths and shortcomings as a family leader. Recognize your strengths - "I am compassionate and committed." Vow to improve on your flaws – "I need to be more consistent with discipline." Try to have reasonable expectations for yourself, your spouse, and your kids. You don't have to have all the answers – be forgiving of yourself. And strive to make parenting a doable job. Focus on the areas that require the greatest attention rather than attempting to solve everything all at once. Admit it when you're worn out. Take time apart from parenting to do activities that will make you joyful.

What does it mean to be wise? is no deal solution. Wisdom is the capacity to make proper judgments in varied conditions. Wisdom is a concept rather than anything real, thus modeling wisdom via examples of excellent, better, and best conduct is the greatest place to begin. Showing your kid the distinction between sensible and incorrect actions — and the repercussions of each — helps him gain a sense of what wisdom looks like. The greatest thing to ask your kid is "was that a sensible decision?" It begins to give kids the impression that adopting the acceptable action is a choice they have. Parents are the finest source to model how to make the correct judgments and intelligent decisions. You may also let them know how you think via your behaviors. pause and think

Teach them to STOP and THINK
When youngsters are taught to pause and ponder they grow up to become mature and responsible people. Every choice whether urgent or not should be properly thought out and effectively conveyed before action is made. The attitude individuals display while making judgments on trivial topics is the same one they will exhibit when making decisions on more serious problems. From the options of what clothing to wear to what University to attend, you can be rest confident that they will always make the appropriate decision.

Set High Standards
Parents should have expectations for their children. Some of these expectations should include their character and their

capacity to make the correct judgments most of the time. When you communicate to them in an inspiring manner and express your conviction in them to choose the correct choices, they grow up with this capacity to know how to think. When you teach your children information, you are instructing them what to think. But when you teach them Wisdom you are teaching them how to obtain their truth.

Share tales to educate youngsters about wisdom and empower them to seek knowledge. The Bible is full of tales that you may share with your children that highlight the significance of being intelligent and making the correct decisions. Solomon is always an excellent example to share with youngsters, when he had the option to ask God for anything, he asked for knowledge. God was so delighted that he added more to him which provided money, status, and success. God places a great premium on intelligence!. Talk to your kid about wisdom in terms of the decisions other characters made and have them offer you their ideas. Ask the question 'was that a sensible decision?" or "what would you have done?"

Teach Them The Power Of Words
Equip your children every day with the truth from the Bible so that they can say the proper words as it affects them and their life. I think there is power in the words that you utter and children may be trained early to assimilate this. Knowledge is also a prayer topic and they may and should ask for God to offer them wisdom regularly to make the proper choice.

Celebrate and Appreciate Their Uniqueness
Every kid is born exceptional, every child is born unique. The first step to teaching a kid originality is that each youngster should be taught to cherish her individuality. No matter their physical makeup whether tall or short, fat or skinny, fair-skinned or dark,

they should cherish who they are. If a youngster doesn't learn to respect him/herself now, she may spend the rest of her life striving to be like someone else. If your kid is not taught early to appreciate and celebrate herself or herself first, then they shouldn't expect anybody else to do so either.

Embrace their Strengths and Work On their Weaknesses

Children should be taught to embrace their strengths (things they are naturally excellent at, have a passion for, or take interest in) and also work on their weaknesses (bad habits and anxieties) (bad habits and fears). As parents, if we can recognize the strengths and shortcomings of our children, we can look at practical strategies to increase their strengths. A youngster that enjoys reading may be fostered with both academic and other resources like periodicals, biographies, journals, etc. Exposure to different topics keeps the youngster balanced and well developed in other areas. On the other side, if the same youngster probably finds it hard to keep his/her room clean, they may be encouraged to obtain a new book if they clean their room regularly or urge them to come up with a creative strategy to get it done.

Have a Positive Attitude

Some youngsters tend to feel highly disheartened when presented with the least obstacle and difficulty. In most situations, it is the attitude when confronted with adversities that might be 'stepping stones to greatness' in disguise. Children should constantly be encouraged to be creative and to discover what they can learn from events and obstacles. For example when a youngster falls do not blame the floor, rather make your child feel better first but then have a conversation with him or her to be more cautious. Refer to Teach your children to Navigate through Life and Circumstances

Ensure Originality

Our students should be taught to consume everything and reflect, devote everything and recover, destroy everything and reconstruct, erase everything and reproduce, determine everything and reply, dismiss everything and remember, sketch everything and relax. These are items that develop distinct individuality qualities in every kid. God is The Source, God is the one who grants creativity and abilities. We should constantly remember that every kid was designed for a particular and unique purpose. The capacity of that kid to connect with his/her God-given destiny will to a considerable measure decide the success of the child. You can never be someone else, be the greatest, you can be.

I CAN Attitude Through Discipline
Any parent who wishes their kid to be triumphant must establish a high degree of discipline and 'I can attitude" in the youngster. Some youngsters are not readily motivated or apathetic about vital concerns that influence their life. When a high degree of discipline is taught to a kid, they will naturally urge themselves to accomplish things and not wait for others to push them.

Take for example a youngster who is expected to accomplish his/her schoolwork. When the kid gets back from school (assuming he or she has been taught a degree of discipline) without being instructed, after eating and relaxing, the next thing will be for them to pick up their school assignments. Another youngster could go directly to the television and be a couch potato. Diligent individuals will always get to the top. This is a crucial lesson about life. Children need to realize that they need much more than simply talent or know-how to be successful, they need to be diligent. Diligent individuals will always get to the top. This is a crucial lesson about life. Children need to realize that they need much more than simply talent or know-how to be successful, they need to be diligent.

parenting tips

Determination
A youngster that will achieve in life must be determined no matter what. While some children are born with a silver spoon in their mouth, others have to strive and work hard for all they earn. No matter the situation of your birth every individual can accomplish what they set their mind to. Having a can-do attitude and the determination to succeed makes all the difference between a child who plays the victim and the one who goes after what he wants.

Humility
The humility being alluded to this is being down to earth at every moment or in every scenario life sends your way. Children need to realize that wherever they are is merely a privilege, not because they are better than anybody else. The only thing to be proud of is hard work and endurance.
Children should learn from an early age to take instructions; corrections and discipline from their parents and instructors. A youngster must also learn to express thanks and appreciation to persons who make contributions to their life. Refer to post- teach them to illustrate 5 stages of teaching children Gratitude

God's Guidance
The most crucial thing you can teach your kid for him/her to succeed in life is the understanding of the fear of God. Some parents prefer to shy away from this extremely important lesson, but the reality is children need to learn that with God on

their side they can accomplish their objectives. All people are born with an inborn sense of the awe of spirituality. Our children should be encouraged to build a personal connection with God. They should establish the practice of submitting everything to God in prayer. Everyone even youngsters must be taught to trust God and not depend exclusively on their ability.

Chapter 6

Using growth mindsets to respond to mistakes and fix them

8 development attitudes that help your kid react to errors and repair them

1. Empower your children to attempt things on their own: As parents, it may be tough to harness our impatience and resist the impulse to take over for our children while they are performing a job. When we do this, though, we unknowingly transmit one of two messages: that they are unable or that we can do it better. Instead, encourage your kid to undertake the activities they can accomplish for themselves - such as getting dressed, cleaning their dish from the table, and so on - to create confidence. When youngsters feel strong, they feel more empowered to undertake new things.

2. Praise effort over results: If you are anything like me, when your kid gives you

their artwork, a knee-jerk reaction is to praise their product with something like, "Wow, this is lovely. You are such a tiny artist. You are the finest painter ever!" From what I discovered more recently, however, when youngsters hear replies that praise what they achieved rather than how hard they worked, it resembles more of an appraisal and they frequently feel pressure to live up to the achievement every time. This may lead to a stuck attitude where the youngster, needs a guarantee, they remain the "best painter ever," avoids painting more complex subjects or attempting new things. By praising the effort, your child feels motivated and proud from within. Here are some things we may do to assist us to celebrate the work of our children:

Comment on what your kid did that was successful: "You continued trying until you got it. I adore how you kept going when things became rough!"

Empathize with the enthusiasm your youngster feels at their achievement: "Wow! You worked incredibly hard on it! I loved seeing you conduct this exercise."
Encourage: "That's a challenging puzzle piece, and I see you trying every place to see where it fits. I believe in you!"
Empower: "That seemed like it was so simple. Let's attempt something tougher to help your brain grow!"
3. Encourage errors and show your mistakes, too: One helpful skill I acquired from Generation Mindful'sTime-In-ToolKit was that errors help me learn and improve. One day, my daughter and I colored the Mistakes Help Me Learn And Grow worksheet that came with the ToolKit. As the tears began to pour in her eyes after her crayon went over the coloring line, we spoke about how our errors are chances to learn and to create something new. And I work on modeling this too. When I make a mistake, I display some grace to myself,

knowing she is watching and learning from my reaction.

4. Model self-encouragement and positive self-talk: Research suggests that youngsters who talk themselves through obstacles remain calmer and can endure when things become tough. Create mantras and positive self-affirmations that your youngster may utilize during periods of frustration. Some of our favorite mantras are:

I am capable of undertaking hard things.
With every breath, I reset.
I can accomplish whatever I think I can.
As your kid learns this sort of self-talk, it becomes an internal reassuring voice to encourage and drive them. Model these affirmations yourself. Your tone becomes their inner voice.

5. Help people identify feelings to manage emotions: You have heard it before - "I am so stupid!" As a parent who loves their kid,

such remarks may damage your heart. Our impulse is to say things like, "You are not dumb. You are clever. Don't speak to yourself that way." Despite our best intentions, this might seem dismissive. Rather than dismissing their sentiments, we may sympathize with them. Saying something like, "you sound incredibly irritated with yourself" might assist put language to the emotion underlying their comment without discounting what they are experiencing.

6. Talk about the brain: The human brain is continually evolving and is dynamic. Teach your youngster about their brain and how errors help us learn and learning helps strengthen our brain muscles.

7. Invite your youngster to ask questions: Teach your youngster to look at faults with a keen eye and ask questions: What would I want to change? What might I add to it? Focus on what they can accomplish instead

of what they can't. Life will undoubtedly toss us curve balls beyond our control, however, we can control how we react and change a problem into a solution.

8. Teach the power of YET: Carol Dweck speaks on the significance of the word yet. When students learn to utilize this three-letter word, it opens doors. The word yet provides children a learning curve, helping them grasp that their talents are not fixed, but rather may be improved with practice and effort. Remember, it isn't what you can't do, it is what you can't do yet. Whether your kids miss a note while playing the piano, strikes out at baseball, color out of the lines, or receive a grade lower than they anticipated, we, as parents, have a fantastic teaching opportunity.

It becomes a moment to honor big feelings surrounding their mistake, and a tool to help them accept and maybe even celebrate it. And most all, we can teach our children that they are cherished and loved as they learn and develop. Teach youngsters about their emotions in entertaining ways!

www.ingramcontent.com/pod-product-compliance
Lightning Source LLC
Chambersburg PA
CBHW070553160726
48003CB00005B/2037